American Art Association

Valuable Antique and Modern Objects of Art, Marble Sculpture, Library Furniture, and Fine Art Books

American Art Association

Valuable Antique and Modern Objects of Art, Marble Sculpture, Library Furniture, and Fine Art Books

ISBN/EAN: 9783744659024

Printed in Europe, USA, Canada, Australia, Japan

Cover: Foto ©Andreas Hilbeck / pixelio.de

More available books at **www.hansebooks.com**

CHARLES H. ROGERS, Esq.

Valuable

Antique and Modern

Objects of Art

AMERICAN ART GALLERIES
MADISON SQUARE SOUTH

No. 80 — MARBLE STATUE, "HUMILITY," ATTRIBUTED TO CANOVA

VALUABLE

ANTIQUE AND MODERN OBJECTS OF ART

MARBLE SCULPTURE
LIBRARY FURNITURE, AND FINE ART BOOKS

TO BE SOLD AT ABSOLUTE PUBLIC SALE
BY ORDER OF THE HEIRS OF THE LATE

CHARLES H. ROGERS, Esq.

FOR MANY YEARS PRESIDENT OF THE
TRADESMEN'S NATIONAL BANK, PHILADELPHIA

ON SATURDAY AFTERNOON, JANUARY 28TH

BEGINNING PROMPTLY AT THREE O'CLOCK

AT THE AMERICAN ART GALLERIES

MADISON SQUARE SOUTH

WHERE THE OBJECTS WILL BE ON EXHIBITION FROM JANUARY 24TH
UNTIL DAY OF SALE, INCLUSIVE

THOMAS E. KIRBY	AMERICAN ART ASSOCIATION
AUCTIONEER	MANAGERS

NEW YORK
1899

CONDITIONS OF SALE.

1. The highest Bidder to be the Buyer, and if any dispute arise between two or more Bidders, the Lot so in dispute shall be immediately put up again and re-sold.

2. The Purchasers to give their names and addresses, and to pay down a cash deposit, or the whole of the Purchase-money, *if required*, in default of which the Lot or Lots so purchased to be immediately put up again and re-sold.

3. The Lots to be taken away at the Buyer's Expense and Risk *upon the conclusion of the Sale*, and the remainder of the Purchase-money to be absolutely paid, or otherwise settled for to the satisfaction of the Auctioneer, on or before delivery ; in default of which the undersigned will not hold themselves responsible if the Lots be lost, stolen, damaged, or destroyed, but they will be left at the sole risk of the Purchaser.

4. *The sale of any Article is not to be set aside on account of any error in the description, or imperfection. All articles are exposed for Public Exhibition one or more days, and are sold just as they are, without recourse.*

5. To prevent inaccuracy in delivery and inconvenience in the settlement of the Purchases, no Lot can, on any account, be removed during the Sale.

6. Upon failure to comply with the above conditions, the money deposited in part payment shall be forfeited; all Lots uncleared within one day from conclusion of Sale shall be re-sold by public or private Sale, without further notice, and the deficiency (if any) attending such re-sale shall be made good by the defaulter at this Sale, together with all charges attending the same. This Condition is without prejudice to the right of the Auctioneer to enforce the contract made at this Sale, without such re-sale, if he thinks fit.

THE AMERICAN ART ASSOCIATION,

MANAGERS.

THOMAS E. KIRBY, *Auctioneer.*

CATALOGUE

1—IVORY TUSK VASE.

> Old Japanese ; finely carved openwork design. " Seven Wise Men in Bamboo Grove." Mounted on carved wood stand incrusted with ivory and lacquers.
>
> Height, 9¼ inches ; diameter, 5 inches.

2—PLAQUE.

> Japanese bronze ; circular shape ; Daimio with Samisen ; wrought in high relief in precious metals.

3—ELEPHANT TUSK.

> With thermometer.
>
> Height, 31 inches.

5

4—AGATE SPHERE.

A perfect specimen.

Diameter, 5 inches.

5—PAIR VASES.

Japanese silver bronze ; inlaid with precious metal ; dragon handles.

Height, 17 inches ; diameter, 9 inches.

6—TRAJAN COLUMN.

Finely wrought in bronze ; black marble base.

Height, 32 inches.

7—OBELISK OF LUXOR.

Finely wrought in bronze ; black marble base.

Height, 52 inches.

8—PAIR BRONZE FIGURES.

Subject, " The Vintage ; " by Devauex, Paris ; black marble bases.

Height, 24 inches.

9—PAIR BRONZE VASES.

Grecian Amphora shape ; classical figures in low relief ; fine green patina.

Height, 22 inches ; diameter, 6 inches.

No. 29—Pair Rare Sèvres Vases

10—Bronze Bust.

Life size; "Rose of May;" by Dumaige, Paris.

Height, 24 inches; diameter, 16 inches.

11—Onyx Pedestal.

Column design; gilt bronze ornaments.

Height, 44¼ inches.

12—Pair Large Vases.

Old Japanese Arita porcelain, decorated with figures, flowers, and other designs in bright colors, with carved wood pedestal.

Height, 26 inches; diameter, 12 inches.

13—Two Hall Vases.

Arita porcelain, cylindrical shape; salmon and gold decoration of figures, flowers, and crests.

Height, 30 inches; diameter, 10 inches.

14—Pair Large Vases.

Old Chinese porcelain, decorated with figures, flowers, and other designs in salmon and gold; bought at The Hague, 1873; with carved walnut and ebonized pedestals.

Height, 32 inches; diameter, 11 inches.

7

15—JAPANESE VASE.

Old Japanese Arita porcelain, decorated with figure and flowers in bright enamels ; scalloped top.

Height, 30 inches.

16—LARGE PLAQUE.

" Mintons " embossed gold ground ; finely painted female head.

Diameter, 20 inches.

17—ELKINGTON PLAQUE.

" The Pompeian Bath ; " from the Centennial Exhibition, Philadelphia, 1876.

Diameter, 20 inches.

18—PORCELAIN PLAQUE.

Decorated by Besche ; subject, " Rainy Day."

Diameter, 20 inches.

19—PAIR PORCELAIN VASES.

Old Mintons ; finely painted decoration of rich plumage birds, flowers, and other designs ; king's blue and gold ground.

Height, 20 inches ; diameter, 12 inches.

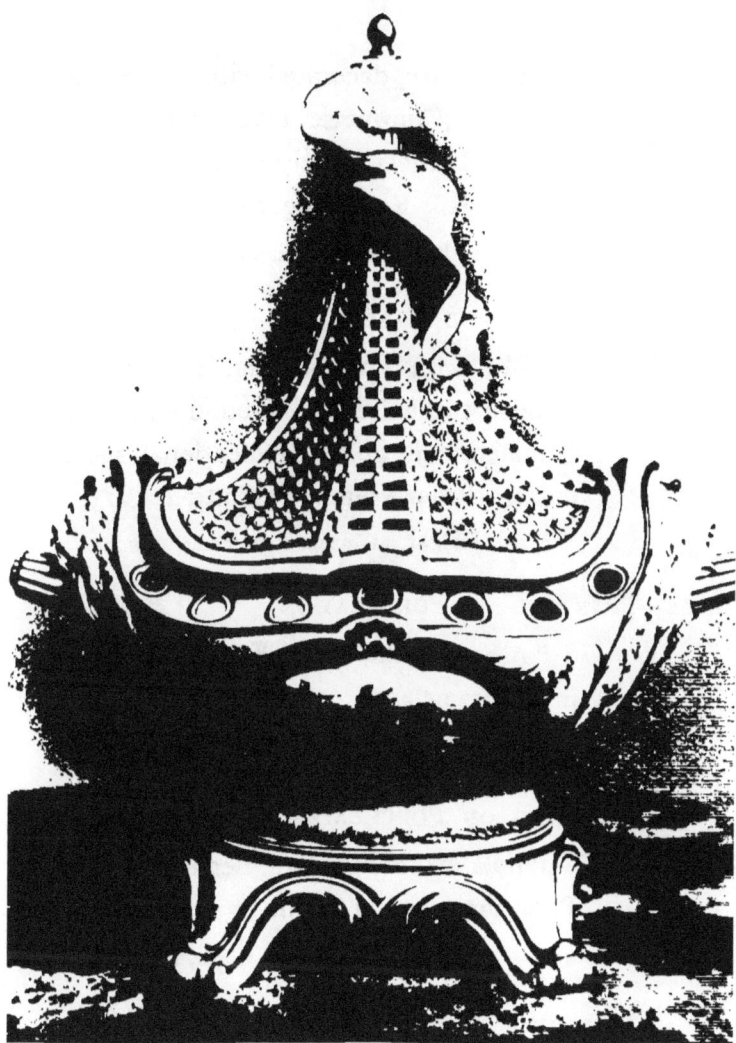

No. 30—The "Ship Vase," Mintons, Stoke-on-Trent

20—SÈVRES VASE.

Pate tendre, decorated with the seasons by Schilt; turquoise blue ground with jewelled borders; finely chiselled ormolu mountings. Exceedingly fine specimen.

Height, 17 inches; diameter, 13½ inches.

21—PAIR COVERED VASES.

"Mintons;" pastoral subjects in four panels; turquoise blue ground and relief ornaments in gold. Exceptional specimens. From Vienna Exhibition, 1873.

Height, 21 inches; diameter, 9 inches.

22—PAINTING ON PORCELAIN.

"A Sick Child," after Knaus; mounted in gilt frame.

Height, 8 inches; length, 10½ inches.

23—PAINTING ON PORCELAIN.

Phiola, "the Venetian Beauty;" after Paris Bordone, by Hohle; gilt frame.

Height, 15 inches; width, 12 inches.

24—PAINTING ON PORCELAIN.

"John Huss. Before the Council at Constance;" after Lessing, by Jahn; mounted in gilt frame.

Height, 24 inches; length, 21 inches.

25—PAINTING ON PORCELAIN.

"Angel of Death ; " after Kaulbach, by Wustlich ; gilt frame.

Height, 15½ inches ; width, 13½ inches.

26—PAINTING ON PORCELAIN.

" Rubens and his First Wife ;" after Rubens, by Langhamer ; gilt frame.

Height, 15 inches ; width, 12 inches.

27—PAINTING ON PORCELAIN.

" Old Sled Maker ; " gilt frame.

Height, 12 inches ; width, 9½ inches.

28—PAINTING ON GLASS.

Copy of Raphael's " Sistine Madonna ;" gilt frame.

Height, 15 inches ; width, 13 inches.

29—PAIR RARE SÈVRES VASES.

Beautiful Etruscan design ; exceedingly fine white texture ; decorated with classical subjects ; artistically painted in Indian red, and pale buff, with gold outlines ; mark of Sèvres factory, 1848. Exceptional specimens.

Height, 16 inches ; diameter, 11 inches.

30—The "Ship Vase."

A superb specimen of Mintons, Stoke-on-Trent. A replica of the celebrated Sèvres vase, formerly in the collection of the late Lord Dudley, and known as the Coventry vase. After the death of Lord Dudley, the vase, together with a pair of fan-shaped ornaments, were sold in London for the sum of £10,000. A replica was also made by Mintons for the Queen, and is now in Buckingham Palace. Decorations: Body color in turquoise blue, relieved by gilding and borders of flowers ; on the obverse is a panel containing a genre subject, and on the reverse one of flowers ; the lid is beautifully reticulated, representing a ship's rigging.

Height, 18¼ inches ; breadth, 15¼ inches.

31—Superb Vase.

Mintons, Stoke - on - Trent. Grecian shape. The obverse, in pâte sur pâte decoration, by L. Solon, represents a nymph "Counselling Cupid to remain faithful, reminding him that this is the wisdom of love." On the balustrade are shown two attendant amourettes ; on the right is a pedestal with a full-length figure of Minerva pointing an arrow ; on the left, an ornamental vase, out of which a luxuriant vine is growing. The reverse shows a group of three amourettes worshipping at the shrine of Minerva, surrounded by rich decorations of feathers, scrolls, and leaves. Body color, peacock blue, with handles, neck, and base richly ornamented with gilding.

Height, 24 inches ; diameter, 9 inches.

32—PAIR GRAND VASES.

Fine Austrian white porcelain, tall ovoid shape ; artistically decorated with figure and landscape subjects by Eugène Poitevin at Sèvres. King's blue ground, with embossed gold ornamentation. From *Exposition Universelle*, Paris, 1879. Have carved wood revolving pedestals.

Height, 54 inches ; diameter, 30 inches.

33—PAIR ELABORATE VASES.

Japanese silver bronze, skillfully wrought and inlaid with gold, silver, and other metals ; relief figures illustrating Japanese mythology ; bold dragon handles. From Centennial Exhibition, Philadelphia, 1876.

Height, 41½ inches ; diameter, 21½ inches.

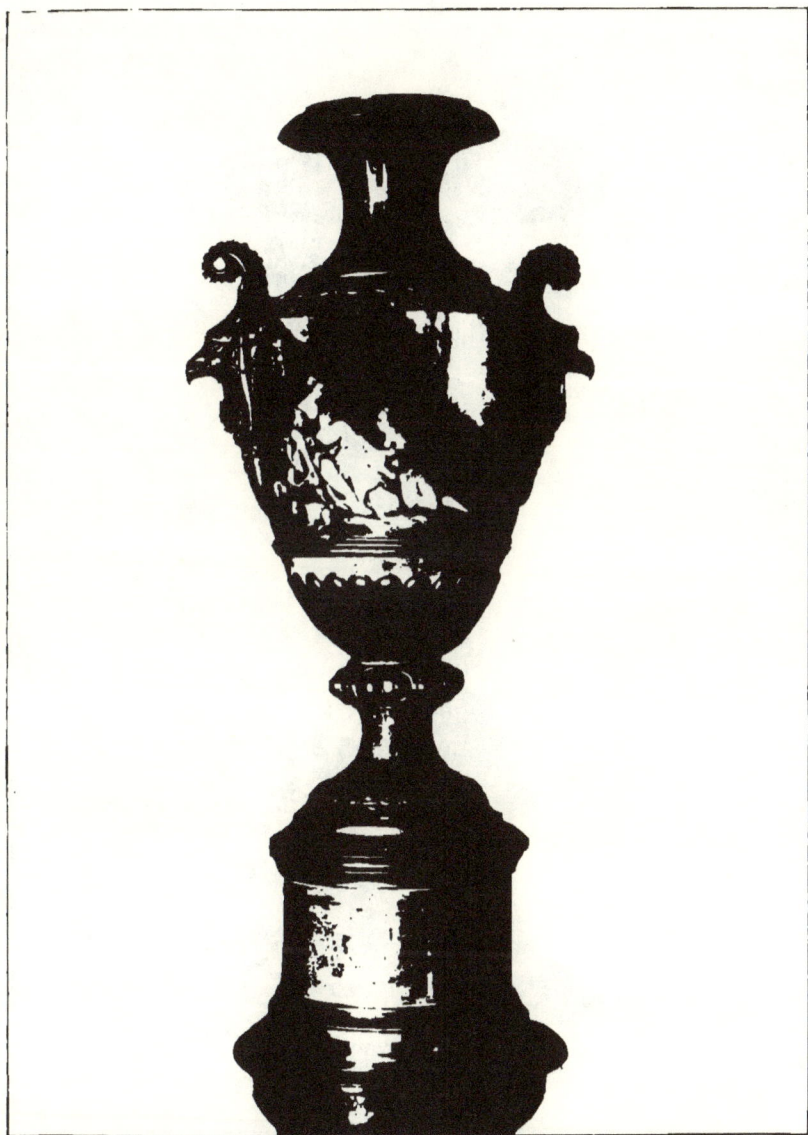

No. 32—One of a Pair of Grand Austrian Vases, Decorated at
Sèvres, by Eugène Poitevin

No. 33—One of a Pair of Elaborate Japanese Silver Bronze Vases

34—PAIR PEDESTALS.

Carved pear wood, made for the foregoing vases.

Height, 29 inches.

35—BRONZE FIGURE.

Benjamin Franklin, by Carrier, Paris.

Height, 25 inches ; width, 11 inches.

36—OAK PEDESTAL.

With enclosure and drawer ; marble
top. Made for the foregoing figure of
Franklin.

Height, 44 inches ; width, 18 inches.

37—BRONZE BUST.

" Femme de Renaissance," by E. Aize-
lin, Paris, 1870.

Height, 21 inches ; width, 10 inches.

38—MARBLE PEDESTAL.

Fluted column design, made for the
foregoing bust.

Height, 44 inches ; diameter, 9 inches.

39—BRONZE GROUP.

" Bacchante ; " cast by Barbedienne,
Paris.

Height, 14 inches ; length, 25 inches.

40—Bronze Bust.

"Cleopatra;" by A. Talquière, Paris.

Height, 27 inches ; width, 17 inches.

41—Bronze Bust.

"Delilah;" by Mercie, Rome, 1871. Cast by Barbedienne, Paris.

Height, 27 inches ; width, 17 inches.

42—Superb Vase.

Wrought in sterling silver and other metals ; repoussé chased ornamentation of birds, blossoms, and berries.

Height, 16 inches ; diameter, 7 inches.

43—Ebonized Pedestal.

Made for the foregoing.

Height, 45 inches ; diameter, 11 inches.

44—Pair Vases.

India onyx ; bronze gilt and oxidized ornaments.

Height, 33 inches ; diameter, 13 inches.

45—Pair Russian Tazzas.

Gold stone and violet jasper, cut and highly polished.

Height, 8 inches ; diameter, 5½ inches.

No. 50—Antique Marble Bas-relief. Cicero

46—Pair Low Pedestals.

Porphyry, cut and highly polished ; black marble bases and tops.

47—Pair Tazzas.

Green jade with violet Russian jasper pedestals ; all finely cut and polished.

Height, 11 inches ; diameter, 8½ inches.

48—Two Small Pedestals.

Lapis lazuli, black marble bases. Antique.

49—Two Tazzas.

Russian rhodonite ; beautifully cut and polished.

Height, 11 inches ; diameter, 9 inches.

50—Antique Bas-relief.

Head of " Cicero." Sculptured in white marble, framed.

Height, 7½ inches ; width, 5 inches.

51—Antique Marble Bas-relief.

Head of " Nero," framed.

Height, 9 inches ; width, 7 inches.

52—Marble Bas-relief.

Oval shape Renaissance head, framed.

Height, 18 inches ; width, 15 inches.

15

53—ANTIQUE MARBLE BAS-RELIEF.

Head of " Cicero," framed.

Height, 18 inches ; width, 15 inches.

54—ANTIQUE MARBLE BAS-RELIEF.

" Worship of Pan ; " black walnut and gilt frame.

Height, 14 inches ; width, 11 inches.

55—ANTIQUE MARBLE BAS-RELIEF.

Head of Emperor Caligula ; walnut and gilt oval frame.

Height, 9½ inches ; width, 8 inches.

56—ANTIQUE MARBLE BAS-RELIEF.

Head of Emperor Vitellius.

Height, 9½ inches ; width, 8 inches.

57—PAIR ANTIQUE LAMACHELLA MARBLE URNS.

Graceful Grecian shape ; grayish violet texture.

Height, 28 inches ; diameter, 8 inches.

58—LARGE ANTIQUE GARDEN URN.

Used as an ornament to tombs ; Pentelic marble ; ornamented in relief with wreaths of flowers, masks, and procession of animals ; found at Hadrian's Villa.

Height, 40 inches ; diameter, 13 inches.

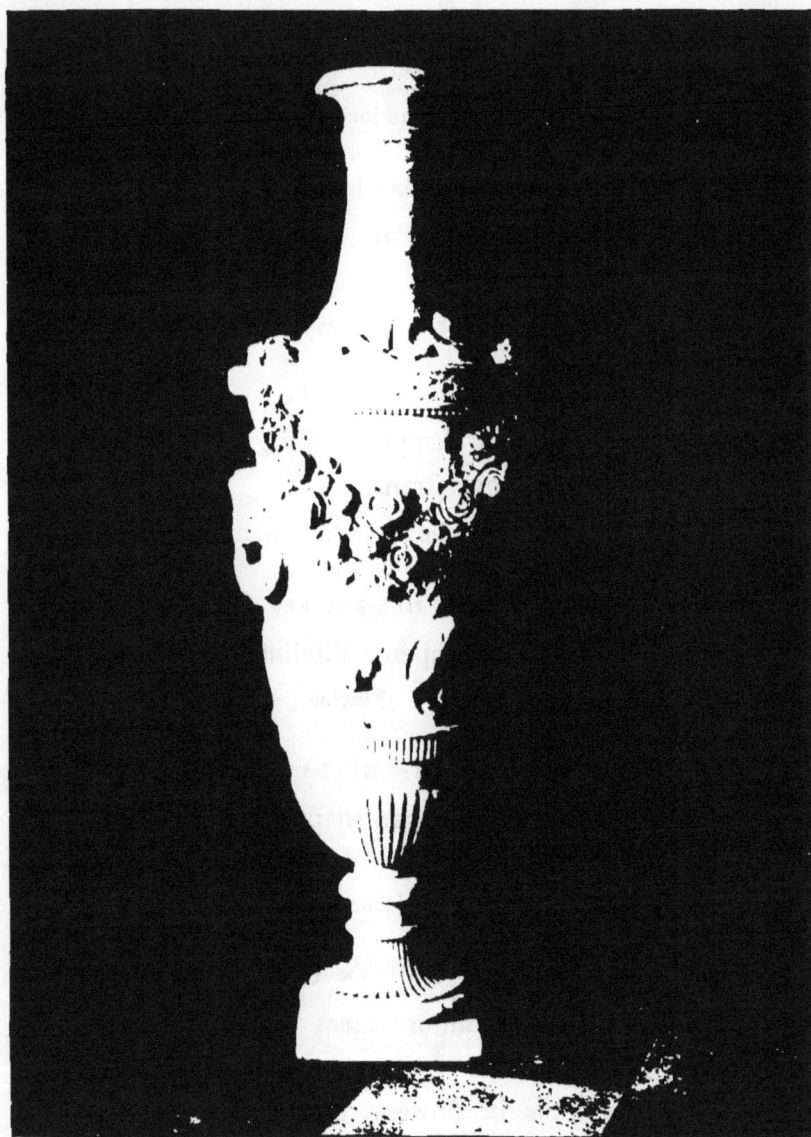

No. 58.—LARGE ANTIQUE GARDEN URN FOUND AT HADRIAN'S VILLA

59—ELABORATE TAZZA.

Oriental red porphyry with base of green antique marble ; finely cut and polished by Leonardi, of Rome, 1874, for the late owner.

Height, 24 inches ; length, 27 inches.

60—LARGE COVERED VASE.

Beautiful urn shape ; Orientaı red porphyry, with base of green and white antique marbles; finely cut and polished by Leonardi, of Rome, 1874, for the late owner.

Height, 30 inches ; diameter, 13 inches.

61—ELABORATE ANTIQUE BARDIGLIO MARBLE PEDESTAL.

Column design, from Herculaneum ; when purchased showed fire marks ; repolished by Leonardi, of Rome. Has giallo antico and African marble base.

Height, 51 inches ; diameter, 11 inches.

62—ELABORATE ANTIQUE PEDESTAL.

Verte antico marble, with base of white and gray marble.

Height, 49 inches ; diameter, 15 inches.

63—Antique Column Pedestal.

>   African marble, with black marble base
>   and top.

>>   Height, 47 inches.

64—Antique Column Pedestal.

>   African marble, with black marble base
>   and top.

>>   Height, 47 inches.

65—Beautiful Jasper Vase.

>   Blood-stone variety ; cut and polished
>   for Mr. Rogers by Leonardi, Rome,
>   from a block of jasper found in the river
>   Tiber; one year was consumed in pro-
>   ducing the vase.   Has base of onyx of
>   antique marble.   A specimen of great
>   rarity and beauty.

>>   Height, 24 inches ; diameter, $8\frac{1}{2}$ inches.

66—Large Tazza.

>   Cut in antique red breccia marble ;
>   oval shape.

>>   Height, 14 inches ; length, 23 inches.

67—Roman Mosaic.

>   Vase of flowers ; beautifully executed
>   by Roccheggiani, Rome, 1874 ; gilt
>   frame.

>>   Height, 27 inches ; width, 22 inches.

No. 65—Beautiful Jasper Vase

No. 71—Antique Marble Bust. Trajan

68—ELABORATE MARBLE TAZZA.

>Verte antico ; very graceful oval shape.
>
>>Height, 15 inches ; length, 20 inches.

69—ANTIQUE MARBLE HEROIC BUST.

>"Scipio," the elder ; excavated at Rome.
>
>>Height, 31 inches ; width, 25 inches.

70—ANTIQUE COLUMN PEDESTAL.

>Beautiful red mottled marble, finely polished.
>
>>Height, 46¼ inches ; diameter, 11 inches.

71—ANTIQUE MARBLE BUST.

>Heroic size ; "Trajan ;" excavated at Rome.
>
>>Height, 34 inches ; width, 24 inches.

72—ELABORATE COLUMN PEDESTAL.

>Antique gray African marble ; cut from a block of marble found in the river Tiber.
>
>>Height, 49¼ inches ; diameter, 11 inches.

73—HEROIC ANTIQUE BUST.

>Sculptured in white marble ; "Claudius ;" excavated in the baths of Caracalla, Rome.
>
>>Height, 35 inches ; width, 25 inches.

74—ANTIQUE COLUMN PEDESTAL.

Cut from a block of Cipollino marble found in the river Tiber; cut and polished by Leonardi, Rome, 1874 ; base of white marble.

Height, 44 inches ; diameter, 11 inches.

75—ANTIQUE MARBLE BUST.

Heroic size ; "Hadrian ; " excavated at Rome.

Height, 37 inches ; width, 25 inches.

76—ANTIQUE COLUMN PEDESTAL.

Cut from a block of reddish marble found in the river Tiber ; cut and polished by Leonardi, Rome, 1874 ; base of African and white marble.

Height, 46 inches ; diameter, 11 inches.

77—COLOSSAL ANTIQUE BUST.

"Augustus Cæsar ; " cut in white marble with yellow onyx drapery ; pedestal of verte antico.

Height, 42 inches ; width, 32 inches.

78—ELABORATE ANTIQUE COLUMN PEDESTAL.

Cut from block of reddish breccia marble found in the river Tiber ; cut and polished by Leonardi, Rome, 1874.

Height, 54 inches ; diameter, 15 inches.

No. 52. Life-size Statue, "Susannah," by G. Lombardi

79—ANTIQUE COLUMN PEDESTAL.

Black-and-white breccia marble, with base of Greek antique marble ; cut from a block found in the river Tiber.

Height, 47½ inches ; diameter, 11 inches.

80—MARBLE STATUE.

Subject, "Humility ; " attributed to Canova ; purchased in Rome, 1874, as a specimen of this famous sculptor's work ; has a modern pedestal, which is composed of various marbles.

Height, 42 inches ; length, 29 inches.

81—HEROIC MARBLE BUST.

Antique, "Silenus," excavated in Rome.

Height, 24 inches ; width, 14 inches.

82—LIFE-SIZE STATUE.

Sculptured in Carrara marble ; subject, "Susannah," by G. Lombardi, Rome, 1874 ; mounted on an elaborate gray marble pedestal, which is ornamented with two bas-reliefs by the same artist.

Height of all, 84 inches ; width, 23 inches.

83—MARBLE STATUE.

Sculptured in Carrara marble ; subject, "Rose of Sharon," by P. Romanelli, of Florence ; has serpentine marble pedestal, with floral festoons carved in relief.

Height of all, 85 inches ; diameter, 26 inches.

P. Romanelli, Professor at Florence, pupil of Bartolini. Among his principal works are : " Monumental Statue of Count Fossombroni," " A Boy Bacchus Treading the Grapes," " The Betrayed," " William Tell's Son " (executed in marble for Mr. Vanderbilt, of New York), a fine portrait " Bust of Bartolini," " The Genius of Italy," " The Nymph of Arno," etc. To the Paris Exposition of 1878 he contributed a statue in marble, " *The Rose of Sharon.*"

84—ELABORATE BRONZE GROUP.

"Perseus and Andromeda," by L. Gregoire ; with bronze and marble pedestal.

Height of all, 81 inches ; diameter, 22 inches.

85—MARBLE GROUP.

Sculptured by Bernini ; subject, " Hercules and Omphale ; " with pedestal composed of various marbles.

Height, 24 inches ; length, 36 inches.

86—BRONZE BUST.

Life-size ; subject, " Cicero ; " copy of original bust in Madrid ; purchased in Rome, 1874.

87—BRONZE BUST.

Life-size; subject, "Demosthenes;" copy of original bust in the Vatican; purchased in Rome, 1874.

88—BRONZE BUST.

Life-size; subject, "Seneca;" copy of original bust in the Louvre; purchased in Rome, 1874.

89—BRONZE BUST.

Life-size; subject, "Marcus Aurelius;" purchased in Rome, 1874.

90—HEROIC BRONZE BUST.

"Hermes."

Height, 30 inches; width, 23 inches.

91—HEROIC BRONZE BUST.

"Venus de Milo."

Height, 30 inches; width, 23 inches.

92—"ARC DE TRIOMPHE."

In bronze; cast by Barbedienne; has black marble base.

Height, 21 inches; width, 20 inches.

23

93—OVAL BAS-RELIEF OF A NEREID.

Antique ; in white marble ; frame of giallo antico and verte antico.

Height, 14¾ inches ; width, 14¾ inches.

94—LARGE LIMOGES VASE.

Cylindrical shape ; lapis lazuli blue glaze, with wild roses, in high relief ; from Paris Exposition, 1878.

Height, 28½ inches ; diameter, 20 inches.

95—LARGE LIMOGES VASE.

Cylindrical shape ; light blue glaze, with water lilies in high relief ; from Paris Exposition, 1878.

Height, 28½ inches ; diameter, 20 inches.

96—PAIR EXTRAORDINARY VASES.

" The Poetry of Pottery ; " manufactured at the Royal Porcelain Works, Worcester, for the Paris Exposition, 1878.

" The processes of the potter's art include so great a variety of scientific, mechanical, and picturesque arrangements, which call forth the artistic powers of the sculptor, the potter, and the painter, that it has seemed desirable to produce an emblematical work in porcelain, which should at once illustrate the past history, together with the future possibilities and triumphs, of ceramic progress.

" With this view a couple of vases have been designed, which illustrate the achievements of the European potter during the

No. 96—ONE OF A PAIR OF EXTRAORDINARY ROYAL WORCESTER VASES,
ILLUSTRATING "THE POETRY OF POTTERY."

" The decoration of pottery in the sixteenth century consisted more in painted sur-
faces than modelled forms. Luca della Robbia, it is true, depended more upon modelling.
The style, however, was peculiar to himself and his family, and his wares constitute but
a very small proportion of the Majolica of the period. The fanciful and elegant designs
of Raphael had stimulated the decorative genius of many artists, and this class of ornament was peculiarly adapted to pottery. There is ample evidence that it was freely used."

sixteenth century, while the verses of Homer and of Longfellow which are introduced make manifest, as it were, the connected record of

   "'The nobility of labour, the long pedigree of toil.'

  "In carrying out this project, assistance has been derived from the work of the gifted Cavaliere Cipriani Picolpasso, who was not only himself a painter of pottery, but the director of the Pottery Manufactory at Castel Durante, during the century above mentioned.

  "The Cavaliere published an account of the various processes employed in the preparation of pottery, and adorned it with drawings, which have enabled succeeding generations to realize most fully the details and associations of the mediæval studio and manufactory.

  "Before, however, proceeding to comment on the vases which have been produced in these modern days at Worcester, in celebration of the glorious and memorable art victories of preceding ages, it may be well to relate first the history and successive stages of the art in various climes, as told by Homer and by Longfellow.

  "Homer's Hymn, 'The Furnace,' 800 B.C.; Longfellow's Poem, 'Kéramos,' 1877, A.D.

  "For the purpose of our story we have selected a series of subjects which have been worked out in alto relievo, to form the decorations of panels, under the following arrangement:—

  "A vase with heads of Luca della Robbia and Maestro Giorgio on the handles.

  "The first panel represents a potter at the wheel, and companion ; while the second shows a modeller and companion.

  "The heads of Michael Angelo and Raphael adorn the second vase, the first panel being a representation of a painter and his companion ; the second illustrating the furnace and the fireman.

  "Michael Angelo and Raphael have been selected as the highest types of Modelling and Painting, and Luca della Robbia and Maestro Giorgio as the representatives of the sister arts directly applied to pottery.

  "Had the poet been aware of our design, he could not have

25

chosen subjects and words better suited to it ; or had the designer first read the verses, it would have been difficult to have selected subjects more adapted for their illustration."

FIRST VASE.

THE POTTER.

BY R. W. BINNS, F.S.A.

Turn, turn, my wheel! Turn round and round
Without a pause, without a sound :
  So spins the flying world away !
This clay, well mixed with marl and sand,
Follows the motion of my hand ;
For some must follow and some command,
  Though all are made of clay !

    *   *   *   *

Like a magician he appeared,
A conjuror without book or beard ;
And while he plied his magic art—
For it was magical to me—
I stood in silence and apart,
And wondered more and more to see
That shapeless, lifeless mass of clay
Rise up to meet the master's hand,
And now contract and now expand,
And even his slightest touch obey.

FIRST VASE.

THE MODELLER.

A nobler title to renown
Is thine, O pleasant Tuscan town,
Seated beside the Arno's stream ;
For Luca della Robbia there
Created forms so wondrous fair
They made thy sovereignty supreme.

26

These choristers with lips of stone,
Whose music is not heard but seen,
Still chant, as from their organ-screen,
Their maker's praise ; nor these alone,
But the more fragile forms of clay,
Hardly less beautiful than they,
These saints and angels that adorn
The walls of hospitals, and tell
The story of good deeds so well
That poverty seems less forlorn,
And life more like a holiday.

SECOND VASE.

THE PAINTER.

Forth from Urbino's gate there came
A youth with the angelic name
Of Raphael, in form and face
Himself angelic, and divine
In arts of colour and design.
From him Francesco Xanto caught
Something of his transcendent grace,
And into fictile fabrics wrought
Suggestions of the master's thought.
Nor less Maestro Giorgio shines
With madre-perl and golden lines
Of arabesques, and interweaves
His birds and fruits and flowers and leaves
About some landscape, shaded brown,
With olive tints on rock and town.

SECOND VASE.

THE FURNACE.

Who is it in the suburbs here,
This Potter, working with such cheer,
In this mean house, this mean attire,
His manly features bronzed with fire,
Whose figulines and rustic wares
Scarce find him bread from day to day?
This madman, as the people say,
Who breaks his tables and his chairs
To feed his furnace fires, nor cares
Who goes unfed if they are fed,
Nor who may live if they are dead?
This alchemist with hollow cheeks,
And sunken, searching eyes, who seeks,
By mingled earths and ores combined
With potency of fire, to find
Some new enamel hard and bright,
His dream, his passion, his delight?

" Longfellow's words embody the requirements of modern times ; it would appear, however, from the fact that Homer addressed his adjuration to Pallas on behalf of the furnace rather than on behalf of the potter and his wares, that he regarded the former as of the higher importance.

" Our modern poet has most justly taken Palissy for his hero, for it is recorded that the one difficulty which more than another tried Palissy's patience and perseverance amid the tears of his wife and the scoffs of his neighbors was " the fire."

" The building of the furnace, the procuring of fuel to fire it, and the difficulty of maintaining the heat—all were special trials for Bernard Palissy. We can fancy him sitting before his oven, and watching with intense anxiety the varying hues of the fire from brown to cherry red, and, higher still, the brighter tones which told of melting power. He consults his hour-glass, and records the time required to raise each special heat, and so ensure successes in the future.

" The vases which form our illustrations have been made at the Royal Porcelain Works, Worcester, for the Paris Exhibition, 1878 ; they are thirty inches in height, and the different branches of art work and manufacture treated of in the story, have been completed by the following craftsmen :—

"*Designer and Modeller*	.	J. HADLEY.
"*Potters*	.	W. FARRINGDON.
		G. RADFORD.
"*Painters and Decorators*	.	J. CALLOWHILL.
		T. CALLOWHILL.
		J. DAVIS.
		T. STEPHENSON.
		W. JONES.
"*Firemen*	.	E. BLAKE, Biscuit.
		T. GOODWIN, Glaze.
		J. GOODWIN, Enamel."

NOTE.—The original pamphlet from which the above extracts have been made will be presented to the purchaser of the vases.

97—ELABORATE LIBRARY CLOCK.

Carved butternut case of Gothic design ; fine movement ; Westminster chimes of eight and ten bells.

Height, 44 inches ; width, 21 inches.

98—OAK CENTRE TABLE.

Top composed of over one hundred specimens of rare and antique stones and marbles ; a key giving the proper name of the various specimens will be presented to the purchaser.

99—CHINESE CENTRE TABLE.

Carved teakwood, and India marble top.

100—FINE ROMAN MOSAIC TABLE.

By C. Roccheggiani, Rome, 1874. Pastoral subject in centre medallion, and surrounded by four panels emblematic of the four seasons ; carved and gilt florentine mounting.

101—ELABORATE ROMAN MOSAIC.

"St. Peters, Rome," by C. Roccheggiani, Rome, 1873 ; mounted in gilt frame.

Height, 31 inches ; length, 61 inches.

102—ELABORATE ROMAN MOSAIC.

"The Forum," by C. Roccheggiani, Rome, 1873 ; mounted in gilt frame.

Height, 31 inches ; length, 61 inches.

103—ELABORATE WOOD CARVING.

Swiss workmanship. Subject : "The Hunters ;" purchased at Berne, 1873 ; on revolving pedestal.

Height of all, 88 inches ; width, 30 inches.

104—FLOWER STAND.

Swiss carving ; relief ornamentation, chickens, turkeys, etc.

105—CONSOL.

>Swiss; elaborately carved; from Berne, 1873.

106—ELABORATE LIBRARY TABLE.

>Carved butternut; has six drawers.

>>Length, 90 inches; width, 47 inches.

107—LARGE LIBRARY SOFA.

>Carved butternut; upholstered in ruby-figured silk plush.

108—LARGE LIBRARY ARMCHAIRS.

>Set of six to match the foregoing sofa.

109—TWO RECEPTION CHAIRS.

>To match the foregoing.

110—ELABORATE LIBRARY DESK.

>Carved butternut.

Length, 6 feet 10 inches; height, 4½ feet; depth, 2 feet 2 inches.

FINE ARTS AND OTHER BOOKS

111—AUDSLEY AND BOWLES. Keramic Art of Japan, with a large number of superb colored plates. 2 vols., folio bound in one, half red morocco. Liverpool, 1865.

112—BINNS (R. W.). Century of Pottery in the City of Worcester, with a History of the Royal Porcelain Works. Numerous illustrations, some colored. 4to, half green morocco. London, 1865.

Large paper copy, only 30 printed.

113—CANOVA (ANTONIO). Works ; in Sculpture and Modelling, with descriptions by the Countess Albrizzi, and a Life of Canova by Cicognara. 154 fine outline engravings by H. Moses, and portrait by Worthington. 3 vols., imperial 8vo, half morocco, gilt top, uncut edges. London, 1849.

114—DULWICH GALLERY. A collection of 50 superb colored plates in imitation of the original paintings, mounted on cardboard, after the pictures by Rembrandt, Claude, Cuyp, Murillo, Salvator Rosa, Teniers, etc. Atlas 4to, half morocco, gilt back.

115—FLORENCE AND PALAIS PITTI GALLERIES.
Over 400 superb engravings of the Paintings, Statuary, Gems, etc., in this famous
collection, with descriptive text. 4 vols.,
imperial folio, green morocco extra, gilt
back, sides, and edges. Paris, 1789.
Brilliant original impressions.

116—HAMILTON (SIR WILLIAM). Collection of
Engravings from Antique Vases; over
200 plates. 3 vols., imperial folio, half red
morocco, gilt back, gilt edges. London,
1791.

117—HAMILTON PALACE COLLECTION. Illustrated
priced catalogue. 4to, cloth. London,
1882.

118—HOPE (T.). Costumes of the Ancients, with
300 fine outline engravings, by H. Moses,
of Egyptian, Greek, Roman, etc., Habits
and Dresses. 2 vols., 4to, Russia extra,
gilt edges. London, 1812.
Large paper copy.

119—JONES (OWEN). Illustrations of the Palace
of the Alhambra, comprising picturesque
views of this famous ancient building, its
apartments, courts, gardens, ornaments, etc.,
with descriptive text; 100 fine colored plates.
2 vols., royal folio, half-red morocco, gilt
back, gilt edges. London, 1842-5.

120—JONES (OWEN). Examples of Chinese ornament. 100 colored plates, folio, cloth. London, 1867.

121—LES ARTS SOMPTUAIRES. Histoire du Costume et de l'Ameublement : par Louandre et Hangard-Maugé : illustrated with a large number of beautifully colored plates. 2 vols., half green morocco. Paris, 1858.

122—PERKINS (C. C.). Tuscan Sculptors ; numerous illustrations. 2 vols., 4to, half morocco. London, 1864.

123—SHAW (H.). Illuminated Ornaments from Manuscripts and Early Printed Books of the Middle Ages ; with descriptive text by Sir F. Madden ; 30 fine colored plates. 4to, half morocco. Pickering, London, 1833.

124—STRAWBERRY HILL. Description of ; illustrated by over 130 plates, many of which are inserted. London, 1798.

> The text is taken from the five-volume edition of Horace Walpole's works, and a leaf in Walpole's autograph is also inserted.

125—TURNER GALLERY. With a portrait of the artist and 60 plates from his best paintings ; proofs on India paper, and a memoir, etc., by Wornum. Folio, half maroon morocco. London, n. d.

126—WARING. Masterpieces of Industrial Art; with a large number of plates, superbly finished in gold, silver, and colors. 3 vols., royal folio, morocco extra, gilt edges. London, 1863.

An illustrated record of famous specimens of metal work, glass painting, etc., etc., in the London Exhibition of 1862.

127—IZU SHICHITO ZENDSU.

"Seven isles of the peninsula of Izu." In three volumes, one volume missing; with hand-colored maps and full illustrations; Japanese text in handwriting; fish and shell-fish beautifully drawn in colors.

128—SCROLL OF "LIFE OF JAPANESE HERO, TAKEDA SHINGEN."

Together with portraits of twenty-four of his distinguished generals, and banner and spear-bearers; all figures excellently drawn and painted in colors.

Takeda Shingen was born in 1521, was the eldest son of lord of Kōshiū. His whole time was spent in waging war against the barons of the neighboring provinces of central and eastern Japan, particularly against Wooyesugi Kenshin, lord of Shinshu. Brave but superstitious, Takeda Shingen was also an adept at governing men.

The scroll was painted in the seventh year of Horeki period (1757).

35

129—DAI NIPPON MEISEKI SHŪ.

A collection of rare and old minerals of Japan. Cuts in hand-painting; Japanese description in handwriting. Dated the tenth year of Kwansei period, ninth month (September, 1798).

THE AMERICAN ART ASSOCIATION,
MANAGERS.

THOMAS E. KIRBY,
AUCTIONEER.

www.ingramcontent.com/pod-product-compliance
Lightning Source LLC
Chambersburg PA
CBHW021555270326
41931CB00009B/1229